FIT FOR A QUEEN

Betty Shamieh

BROADWAY PLAY PUBLISHING INC
New York
www.broadwayplaypub.com
info@broadwayplaypub.com

Cover photo by Lelund Durond Thompson

First edition: April 2018
I S B N: 978-0-88145-763-6

Book design: Marie Donovan
Page make-up: Adobe InDesign
Typeface: Palatino

FIT FOR A QUEEN was first produced by the Classical Theatre of Harlem (Ty Jones, Artistic Director; David Roberts, Managing Director) opening on 7 October 2016. The cast and creative contributors were:

SENENMUT..Sheria Irving
WANRE .... John Clarence Stewart
HATSHEPSUT ....April Yvette Thompson
NEFERURE.. Shereen Macklin
THUTMOSE II .... Gilbert Cruz
TUTU (THUTMOSE III)................................ Eshan Bay
MERITRE.. Sujotta Pace
Ensemble .... Kalon Hayward
Ensemble ....Nedra Snipes
Ensemble .... Portland Thomas
Ensemble .... Tiffany Nicole Webb

Director.. Tamilla Woodard
Choreography...Joya Powell
Set design............... Christopher Swader & Justin Swader
Costume design....................................Rachel Dozier-Ezell
Lighting design .... Alan C Edwards
Sound design.................................... Hillary Charnas
Sound engineer .... Brad Ward
Props master ....William Farmer
Stage management .... Chelsea Friday
Production manager ....Joshua Kohler
Assistant director....................Lelund Durond Thompson
Assistant stage manager ....Halle Morse
Production assistant .... Lamar Perry
Master electrician ....Ryan Jacobsen

For Muna and Basem Hishmeh, with my thanks

NOTE

The main characters are inspired by individuals who lived during the New Kingdom era of ancient Egypt.

CHARACTERS

SENENMUT, *a slave girl*
WANRE, *a scribe*
HATSHEPSUT, *a queen who becomes pharaoh*
NEFERURE, HATSHEPSUT's *daughter*
THUTMOSE II, HATSHEPSUT's *husband*
TUTU (THUTMOSE III), NERFERURE's *husband*
MERITRE, *a harem girl*

Casting requirements: 4 females, 3 males

Scene 1

(Setting: a garden outside the palace. SENENMUT *is waiting anxiously.)*

SENENMUT: Where have you been?

*(W*ANRE *enters and approaches* SENENMUT.*)*

WANRE: Looking for you, my love. I've been wandering the garden for hours. I almost went home.

SENENMUT: *(Embracing him)* Shut up and hold me. How dare you talk about going home? Say it again and I'll have Happy execute you.

WANRE: Do not joke around.

SENENMUT: I'm not joking.

WANRE: You are four hours late. What was I supposed to do?

SENENMUT: Wait for me, of course. It was a horrible night. Horrible. Happy stayed up late, talking, talking, talking—

WANRE: *(Holding her)* And you are still completely in Queen Hatshepsut's favor?

SENENMUT: Dare you ask such a question?

WANRE: Did you ask the Queen about making me head scribe yet?

SENENMUT: We make love now, we make you head scribe later.

WANRE: So you can make me head scribe?

SENENMUT: I can do much more than that. Watch. There are many changes about to happen in the royal household. Changes that will make it so we can be together more often. Maybe every night. The pharaoh Thutmose is ill. He'll die shortly. And my mistress will take the throne after him. She is to be the next pharaoh.

WANRE: A woman cannot be a pharaoh, a god on earth.

SENENMUT: Then, why have the past two pharaohs only left daughters behind them to rule? What do the gods expect us to do?

WANRE: I do not know.

SENENMUT: Well, do yourself a favor and pretend that you do. As head scribe, you'll be expected to answer such questions. And you do clearly desire that I help you get the position of head scribe, don't you, my love? Is that not why you've come?

WANRE: No. I hope my merits alone will get me where I need to go. However, a kind word floating from your lips to Queen Hatshepsut's ears could do no harm.

SENENMUT: I'll think about it. But first you must convince me of your...merits.

WANRE: Now, now. Senenmut, my sweet, we need to have a little talk. Last night was lovely, but I don't think it's a good idea to meet again, my dear and honorable Senenmut.

SENENMUT: What?

WANRE: You are Queen Hatshepsut's favored servant. You are required to be a virgin.

SENENMUT: I'm still a virgin. Technically.

WANRE: If we are found out, I would be killed instantly. Queen Hatshepsut would be sure of that.

SENENMUT: What of it?

WANRE: You know I would die for you. But I have a family. Who would take care of them?

SENENMUT: Families are so convenient to men. So easily forgotten and so suddenly remembered.

WANRE: I have children.

SENENMUT: Do you think I care for your children? Your wife?

WANRE: Senenmut, you know I adore you, but we can't go on like this. This loving that is not love-making, sex that is almost sex. What kind of fool am I to chose a sworn virgin for my lover?

SENENMUT: I chose you.

WANRE: Of course you did but I also chose—

SENENMUT: No. I chose you. Don't forget that. The woman always chooses. The only question is whether she lets the man think so or not.

WANRE: Okay. Look, I'm going to cause you nothing but trouble. What right do I have over Queen Hatshepsut's favored servant and maiden?

SENENMUT: The right I give you. Trust me. Happy does everything I tell her. I play her like a harp and, with my touch, I keep that woman humming long after I leave her—

WANRE: Is that so? Then win the right to make yourself my lover.

SENENMUT: She's a harp that's a bit out of tune. Old-fashioned. She wants me for herself alone and, when she dies, I die with her so I can serve her in death. That is all she asks.

WANRE: That is all? Only giving up sex and life?

SENENMUT: But she gives me such power in return. All worldly pleasures are mine, except for those a women gets from a man. *(Pause)* And, yet, I think I got the unlucky deal. No more talking. Quickly hold me before I have to return to Happy's side.

WANRE: No. It's time to say good-bye. I'll think of you often, but I won't come back again.

SENENMUT: You will come back.

WANRE: No, Senenmut. I will not.

SENENMUT: You will.

WANRE: Listen, I'm sure I can get the job by myself. I'm a better scribe than you give me credit for. Good-bye, Senenmut. If you don't think I deserve it, you don't have to recommend me for the position.

SENENMUT: You will do exactly as I tell you or you and your precious family won't live to see another dawn, I swear it. You were working on Thutmose's pyramid, were you not, when ink was spilt and a whole year's work was lost?

WANRE: Yes, but I was not working that day—

SENENMUT: I can tell my mistress you were responsible.

WANRE: You wouldn't!

SENENMUT: I would and you will not interrupt me again. Thank you. I can tell her you did that. I can tell her you hate Re and the gods. I can tell her I don't like the color of your robe and she will kill you and your family. In any gruesome manner I desire. To please me.

WANRE: No!

SENENMUT: Yes! So you will come back when I deem it so. And you'll give up your work, your family, or anything that you must to be here when I call, until I tire of you. Which will not be soon. Don't you worry, my love, my Wanre. Happy chose me and I choose you for your beauty. How does it feel? To know you'll come back every time I call because, simply because, I like you. Everything about you. Even the shape of the shadow your body makes entices me.

WANRE: You would kill me! I, who loves you more than anyone—

SENENMUT: Spare me. You had your chance to make this exchange about love. *(Holding him)* Now do your duty and do it like a man. Take me to the edge of what my vow allows.

Scene 2

(Setting: It is day and we are inside the palace banquet room. SENENMUT *is on-stage.* HATSHEPSUT *enters.)*

HATSHEPSUT: Senenmut! Senenmut!

SENENMUT: Hello to you too, Happy. Did you sleep well?

HATSHEPSUT: Not so good. I had a rather disturbing dream. Would you like to hear about it?

SENENMUT: Of course, Happy. What did you dream about?

HATSHEPSUT: Oh. You don't want to hear about my dreams, do you? You probably think I talk too much anyway.

SENENMUT: You do. But I love it and wouldn't have it any other way. I could listen to you for the rest of my life.

HATSHEPSUT: And you will, because, you and I, we'll only live as long as the other lasts. Tell me, Senenmut, how was your night?

SENENMUT: Fine as usual. Come on, Happy. What did you dream about?

HATSHEPSUT: Well, I dreamt…no, you don't really care to hear about this dream.

SENENMUT: Happy, tell me your dream.

HATSHEPSUT: If you insist, I had a dream that you weren't sleeping in your bed last night.

SENENMUT: Oh?

HATSHEPSUT: Yes, it was very odd. In my dream, you snuck out into the garden.

SENENMUT: Uh huh.

HATSHEPSUT: And you met a man there.

SENENMUT: I see.

HATSHEPSUT: And you exchanged words and kissed and touched and got into some very interesting positions and then you came running back to the palace and arrived here just a few moments ago.

SENENMUT: Happy, I—

HATSHEPSUT: Enough! I don't want to hear your lies, and no lover ever wants to hear the truth. Now you know I should scold you, but I'm so relieved that you didn't try to run off that I can hardly care. If you did not love me so, you would have, knowing I would be forced to kill you. You know I would kill you, don't you?

SENENMUT: I know.

HATSHEPSUT: Oh, don't pout, Senenmut. Please. You know how I hate it when you look down.

SENENMUT: Sorry.

HATSHEPSUT: Are you mad at the slave who spied on you and followed you into the garden?

SENENMUT: Yes.

HATSHEPSUT: Would you like me to kill him?

SENENMUT: Yes.

HATSHEPSUT: How?

SENENMUT: Any which way, just as long as I can watch.

HATSHEPSUT: You're so bad. I won't execute a man for spying on you. Then, no one else would offer to take that job next. And obviously I need eyes on you at all times.

SENENMUT: Don't execute him for spying on me. Execute him for spying on you. Was it not Tertamun who told you I had left your chamber?

HATSHEPSUT: Maybe.

SENENMUT: Did Tertamun volunteer to spy on me? Out of the blue? Or did you ask it of him?

HATSHEPSUT: What does it matter?

SENENMUT: He's your daughter's favorite servant.

HATSHEPSUT: So?

SENENMUT: So why is he not with your daughter? It's clear she sent him here to spy, to cause trouble between us, to drive us apart.

HATSHEPSUT: You're the one driving us apart.

SENENMUT: You know the real reason why I fooled around with that man, don't you?

HATSHEPSUT: Because you wanted to?

SENENMUT: No. Because I'm just preparing myself emotionally for the dreaded day you'll have to share me.

HATSHEPSUT: Share you?

SENENMUT: Yes, you know when your daughter's husband ascends to the throne. Who knows what will happen? Only a pharaoh has absolute power and it's been said that Tutu humps anything that moves. Did he not dare to give a command that I should be sent to serve him if you tire of me?

HATSHEPSUT: And I told him personally I never would. I made it very clear he was to keep his eyes and hands off my servants.

SENENMUT: And you think that will stop him when he is a pharaoh? It must be lovely. To go around believing people will always obey you in the future because they have done so in the past.

HATSHEPSUT: Tutu would never cross me. The scribes say, if my husband dies soon, I will rule as regent. Tutu is not the son of a pharaoh, he'll need me as a royal advisor.

SENENMUT: For a time, yes. But, if he becomes pharaoh, he will be a pharaoh over everyone. Over you. Over me. But, there's nothing I can do except pray about it. So, I do. I pray the great goddess Isis will make you see that there are priestesses all over Egypt who would support the idea of a female pharaoh. Powerful [priestesses!]—

HATSHEPSUT: Don't start this again.

SENENMUT: This is the third time a son-in-law will be chosen instead of the rightful heir simply because she is a woman.

HATSHEPSUT: I know. Pity.

SENENMUT: It is a crime against nature and against the cunning Mistress of Magic Isis. What about the women who come after you?

HATSHEPSUT: I said it was a pity. But must we worry about everyone else's troubles all the time? I'm tired of unhappiness. I will not ignore the gods' gifts. I have been given musicians who drum rhythms for dancers, dancers to give those rhythms life, and, at last, you. Who makes all that beauty matter.

SENENMUT: Those that stay completely content with what they have end up losing it. Tertamun was sent here to cause discord between us. Show your servants what happens if they dare to meddle in your affairs, even on the orders of other royals. Kill Tertamun.

HATSHEPSUT: I will not have it known I kill those who spy on you for me.

SENENMUT: Then, don't give a reason for why he is to be killed. Just have him killed.

HATSHEPSUT: *(To a servant off-stage)* Behead Tertamun. *(To* SENENMUT*)* He always seems to enjoy telling me unkind things about you. It's like he gets a kick out of it.

SENENMUT: Why would he not? Servants often dream of seeing their betters suffer. You don't know it because you've never had to serve anyone. You think people are kind because you are kind. You think people wish the best for you because you wish the best for them. But, the world is not made up of people like you, Happy. It's made up of people like—

NEFERURE: *(Off-stage)* Mother! *(She enters.)* Mother! Why have you sentenced my henchman Tertamun to death? Without giving him a chance to speak? Without my consent?

HATSHEPSUT: Um, I…

SENENMUT: He's been sentenced for a transgression against the gods. It is said that he has questioned the existence of the god Thoth in every ibis.

NEFERURE: We all question that. Now if he is guilty of a religious transgression, then let the gods he sinned against strike him down. I will not stand for injustice. I will go to Father.

SENENMUT: My dear girl, you don't want to disturb your father with the life of a lowly scribe—

NEFERURE: The lowest scribe is higher born than you! It's amazing to see how well you've learned to speak proper Egyptian, so we royalty won't feel uncomfortable around you. It's a smart slave's trick. One could almost forget you started out cleaning the shit of the animals.

HATSHEPSUT: Do not speak that way to Senenmut. You know I have given her the title of "great tutor." Your tutor.

NEFERURE: Mother!

HATSHEPSUT: Daughter, you seem extraordinarily concerned with the fate of this servant, Tertamun. Why?

NEFERURE: Tertamun is everything a servant should be. He is loyal and faithful. He heeds my every command.

HATSHEPSUT: What kind of commands? Commands like hang about the Queen's chamber and meddle in affairs that don't concern him? Commands like that?

NEFERURE: No. Um. No. Okay, so what? Maybe I asked him to check on you, Mother, to make sure you were doing well and not being taken advantage of by those in your inner circle. He doesn't deserve to die for that.

HATSHEPSUT: I think he does. I think you both need to be taught a lesson. I have ordered what I have ordered. Daughter, you are dismissed.

NEFERURE: I'm not leaving, Mother!

SENENMUT: As your tutor, it's my duty to school you in the ways of the world. Leave our chamber now. Stay any longer and she might kill another of your favored servants, like Wareset, to teach you manners. It's really best to be rational.

NEFERURE: Servants should only speak when spoken to.

HATSHEPSUT: Then I should too. Because in my heart, I serve my Senenmut.

NEFERURE: Mother, I don't care whose feet you want to lick as long as you don't step on my toes. I order you to take back your order.

HATSHEPSUT: Did I miss something? Did you suddenly become pharaoh? Because last time I checked, only the pharaoh has absolute power. If you care for this servant so much, you have my permission to give him a burial that is above his station in life. Prepare for him the blessed map he'll need in the afterlife.

NEFERURE: Mother, you have not heard the last of this. *(She exits.)*

HATSHEPSUT: She really is a terrible bore, isn't she?

SENENMUT: No. Not at all.

HATSHEPSUT: Oh, I know you're only trying to spare my feelings. But I know what she is. That girl will drive me to my death. How am I supposed to love something that looks exactly like my mother-in-law. If only we could pick who we wanted in our families. Senenbutty…

SENENMUT: Yes, Happy?

HATSHEPSUT: Feel like going into my chamber?

SENENMUT: As you wish. I am your humble servant, my Queen.

HATSHEPSUT: Don't call me that and don't say it like that. You know how I hate it when you make it sound as if you don't love me.

SENENMUT: You will spare the life of the scribe Wanre, won't you, Happy? I just happened to meet him in the garden last night when I was taking a midnight stroll. He didn't know I was your servant.

HATSHEPSUT: Why would I want to harm him? I would never do a thing like that.

SENENMUT: Please, Happy. Check your rage.

HATSHEPSUT: Am I so transparent?

SENENMUT: *(Nods)* He didn't know I was your servant.

HATSHEPSUT: Well, he's going to learn. The very hard way. He is my son-in-law's favorite scribe, but he has to die.

SENENMUT: Is there nothing I can say to dissuade you, Happy? Oh, well! Behead him if you feel like it. What do I care?

Scene 3

(THUTMOSE II *is lying leisurely in his chamber, with* MERITRE *attending him.* NEFERURE *enters.*)

NEFERURE: Father, I must talk to you in private.

THUTMOSE II: We are in private, darling.

NEFERURE: Father, dismiss the servant.

THUTMOSE II: Why?

NEFERURE: Because I must talk to you in private.

THUTMOSE II: Everyone always comes in here demanding things. And today of all days, I'm so tired. I'm so tired today.

NEFERURE: I wish it were your last day.

THUTMOSE II: What?

NEFERURE: To be tired, of course. As your only daughter, I demand to speak to you in private.

THUTMOSE II: You demand of me?! I am the pharaoh! I am the tip that makes the pyramid's top point to heaven, the rise that makes the river Nile run, the handle of the shooting star's knife that slices white lines of light into the night—

NEFERURE: Enough already! Leave, servant! Do you understand orders? *(Pointing to Meritre)* Well, if it isn't my good friend Buck-tooth! Hey, Buck-tooth! Are you too stupid to understand Egyptian? I said, get out!

THUTMOSE II: Don't listen to her. You have no right to speak to my servants like that.

NEFERURE: Get out!

MERITRE: I understand Egyptian, madam. I'm waiting for orders from the pharaoh.

NEFERURE: Get out!

(MERITRE exits.)

NEFERURE: Mother has ordered the death of Tertamun.

THUTMOSE II: What?

NEFERURE: Mother has—

THUTMOSE II: You've kicked out my slave to plead the life of a servant your mother wants dead? Are you crazy? You know I'm not one to stand in your mother's way. We stay out of each other's business.

NEFERURE: Tertamun is not just any servant, but a trusted friend. I want him to serve me in the afterlife.

THUTMOSE II: How old is he?

NEFERURE: Forty.

THUTMOSE II: That's time enough for him in this world. Call in the dancers on your way out.

NEFERURE: Father, Mother has gone completely out of control. If she wanted Tertamun dead, I would not object. But it's all because of that horrible little whore Senenmut. Tertamun is a righteous man. He taught me how to read. I will not stand for this.

THUTMOSE II: You can't read. We pay the scribes to read for us. We don't learn ourselves.

NEFERURE: But, I did, remember? Mother insisted.

THUTMOSE II: See, you see, what a loving, doting, warm, gentle and sentimental woman your mother is. She knows what's best. I'll not stand in her way.

NEFERURE: I fear what she is capable of.

THUTMOSE II: That makes two of us.

NEFERURE: What if she marries again? I mean, if anything were to happen to you.

THUTMOSE II: Happen to me? Nothing is going to happen to me. You can be sure of that. I am the pharaoh!

NEFERURE: You are going to die someday. It's best to plan ahead.

THUTMOSE II: Who told you about that cough of mine? Was it your mother?

NEFERURE: Father.

THUTMOSE II: Don't call me father. You are no daughter of mine. Trying to get me into trouble with Hatshepsut.

NEFERURE: Father, listen. I'm just saying it's better to plan. Let's say you won't die, the laws of nature will change just for you. One day, the gods will ride down on golden chariots to pick you up and make you one of the kings of heaven!

THUTMOSE II: Now that's more likely. What a fine idea! I think I'll have that engraved in stone. Because I am the pharaoh! The mighty pharaoh! The mightiest of the mighty—

NEFERURE: Pharaohs! Now say we are left here on earth without our great pharaoh, who would be here to replace you?

THUTMOSE II: Oh, I see.

NEFERURE: Right. Now naturally, you would want one of your glorious offspring to take over, no? So that the wonder of your days would live on through us.

THUTMOSE II: No actually. I really don't give a sparrow's shit for what happens to the rest of you.

NEFERURE: Father! You don't want the other pharaohs in heaven to laugh at you. Remember that your right to rule is only because you married Mother. It is she who is the daughter of the last pharaoh, remember? So her right to the throne will be bestowed on anyone else she chooses to marry...

THUTMOSE II: You're right. What am I going to do?

NEFERURE: You are going to make sure that I, your only descendent, will pass the rule to my children.

THUTMOSE II: How will I do that?

NEFERURE: You will name my husband Thutmose III as the next pharaoh. If Mother has no intention of remarrying—

THUTMOSE II: She would never. Besides, it's obvious I'll outlive the both of you.

NEFERURE: That's true, Father. But I just want to ensure you get all the heaven you want in the afterlife.

THUTMOSE II: Well...even if I do ascend to heavens and to my place among the gods, I don't think Hatshepsut will try to remarry. She has always preferred the company of women.

NEFERURE: Father, you must do this! For your own sake.

THUTMOSE II: We may still beget a son.

NEFERURE: Father, we all know you have been incapable for years.

THUTMOSE II: How do you know?

NEFERURE: We all know.

THUTMOSE II: Well, then…how dare you say you know?

NEFERURE: Everybody knows.

THUTMOSE II: I am not impotent!

NEFERURE: If you say so. But the doctors have been saying for months that you are on your deathbed.

THUTMOSE II: Lies! Lies! Call them in here.

NEFERURE: I will! But only after you send for the high priests to meet us in your chamber at dawn.

THUTMOSE II: Dawn? Dawn is very early.

NEFERURE: Dawn is the earliest every high priest from every corner of Egypt can make it here. They are to be witnesses to you swearing the royal oath naming my husband the next pharaoh who is ready to rule without the help of a regent. Send for them now, Father! Or I won't leave.

THUTMOSE II: What do you mean 'you won't leave?' I am the pharaoh. The mighty pharaoh! I am the son of Osiris and brother of Horus! Okay, okay, but don't tell your mother about this till I, you know, ascend to the heavens on golden chariots to take my place among the gods et cetera, et cetera. Because if I'm not dead when she finds out, she will make me wish I were.

Scene 4

(The stage should be split into two spaces, with the light focusing alternately on the two separate actions that are going on. In each of the two spaces, there should be a bathtub. In one space is MERITRE *preparing a bath. In the other space, it is* WANRE *preparing a bath.* SENENMUT *enters into* MERITRE'S *space.)*

SENENMUT: Moonbeam, how are you? It's been years!

MERITRE: Fine, Senenmut. Fine. You know how I
always hated that nickname. So you're the royal I'm
supposed to give a bath to! Who would believe it? I
heard Queen Hatshepsut gave you the title of "great
tutor." O great tutor, teach me something.

SENENMUT: What do you want me to teach you?

MERITRE: How you got yourself such a sweet deal?
Everyone at home is real proud of you. The palace is a
far cry from the Temple of Isis.

SENENMUT: It's a day job, you know. Pays the bills.
What have you been up to?

MERITRE: Been working the harem.

SENENMUT: Really? Well, hop in the tub. Today, I'll
give you the royal treatment. And tell me about your
life, the harem, everything. You know that would have
been my route if Happy hadn't chosen me.

(*Lights go down on* SENENMUT *and* MERITRE. SENENMUT
can continue giving MERITRE *a bath or they can freeze.
Lights up on* TUTU *entering where* WANRE *is drawing a
bath. We can now see that* WANRE *is dressed as a woman.*)

WANRE: Tutu, you probably don't know who I am,
but—

TUTU: Hi, Wanre.

WANRE: Do you recognize me?

TUTU: Of course, my clever Wanre. After all this time,
you know I can recognize you from almost every angle.

WANRE: I need your help, Sire. I've angered Queen
Hatshepsut, and I fear for my life. I was forced to
submit to Senenmut's demands—

TUTU: Why would someone of your class worry about a slave? Especially a woman? There is nothing lower in the world. You have to learn to show them their place.

(The lights go down on TUTU *and* WANRE, *and up on* SENENMUT *scrubbing* MERITRE's *back.)*

MERITRE: What's life in the harem like? Well, we women sleep outside most nights. Alone, where the balmy wind blows upon me. I pretend it is a lover's breath. Soft, unexpected. Times are hard. During the day, if I'm not attending to the pharaoh, I work the land alongside the men. There's only one pharaoh and he always has his favorites. But he never visits even the favorites anymore. Because he's sick, of course. they remind him of his more virile days. I never was one, a favorite, on account of my buck teeth. *(Senenmut stops scrubbing in order to listen)* He told me they made me seem ugly to him and to keep my mouth closed to cover them when he was around. So I tried to. But the last time he took me, it hurt so much, I cried out. He stopped in the middle of it all. He walked away as if he was going to leave. But then he paused, naked in the doorway, and he came back to me and told me to get up and open my mouth. When I did, he leaned towards me, his eyes never wavering from mine. And I tried not to blink because it seemed like...no, I am sure of it, he wasn't blinking. He cleared his throat and spit into my mouth and told me to swallow. Then he left. He mostly ignores me now, but I think I like it better that way.

(Pause)

SENENMUT: You'll see what I'm going to do to that man, Moonbeam. You're going to live to see the pharaoh get his due for what he did to you.

MERITRE: Oh, it doesn't bother me much. I mean, I don't get jewelry like some favorites do. I'd like to

have that to give to my daughter, in case something
happened to me and I couldn't take care of her.

SENENMUT: (*Taking off jewels and putting them on*
MERITRE) I'm making you my own favorite. You'll
see, I'm going to kill him and make Happy the next
pharaoh.

MERITRE: You can kill him, but Queen Hatshepsut isn't
going to be the next pharaoh.

SENENMUT: What?

MERITRE: You mean, you haven't heard?

(The lights shift to WANRE *and* TUTU.)

WANRE: Senenmut has told me about her plans to
make Hatshepsut usurp your rights and become the
next pharaoh.

TUTU: I'm not interested in what a crazy slave has to
say, though I must say she is quite a woman. It's really
so unbecoming of Hatshepsut to refuse to share her
with me for a night or two. Should I banish from my
sight any slave girl who isn't as pleasing to look upon?
What do you think?

WANRE: That's your choice, Sire. With your permission,
I hope to flee Egypt to save my life. I can go to Syria.
I have friends there. Please look after my wife and
children, protect them from her.

TUTU: Is that all you want? I assure you they'll be safe
from this slave girl you fear.

WANRE: And look after yourself. Sire, as your scribe, I
must advise you to be careful. Your claim to the throne
is not secure, since you are not the son of a pharaoh.
Remember that twice in our history a woman has
headed our country. As regents, mere advisors, but
nevertheless women have been at the helm of the great
ship that is Egypt. It can happen again. It's better to

learn from the examples of the past, Sire, before you
become one.

TUTU: I'm more concerned with the future, which
hopefully includes having a relaxing bath. I've had a
hard day planting those new tulips from Canaan in my
garden. I don't want to hear another unpleasant word.
Especially about a slave, slaves are like the worms in
my garden that I crush at my feet. *(Wagging his finger as
Wanre attempts to speak)* Not another word!

(Lights shift to MERITRE *and* SENENMUT.*)*

SENENMUT: Tell me everything. You have nothing to
fear. Royals are like worms I wrap around my finger.

MERITRE: All I can say is the princess Neferure came
by and spoke to the pharaoh earlier. Some of us girls
eavesdropped at the door. I shouldn't say anything
else. I've got my kid to think about and I could get in
trouble. The princess is already angry with me because
her husband gives me longing looks once in a while.

SENENMUT: No, Moonbeam, trust me. I'm turning this
palace upside down and soon you'll have your own
harem. You and I will be having our own favorites
then! Rumps piled up, for the picking and for the
plucking. By the bundles, like fruit at the market. Lines
upon lines of behinds, stacked and roped like grapes
on a vine.

MERITRE: I don't know about all that—

SENENMUT: Have I ever gotten you in trouble for going
along with my schemes? Even when we were eight and
we stole gold statues from the temple and tried to trade
it for licorice at the marketplace? What did I do?

MERITRE: You were whipped like a dog by the priest
Maatre, almost to death, but you never told on me. You
insisted that you did it alone.

SENENMUT: Right. And Maatre? What ever happened to him?

MERITRE: Maatre died when a huge brick being taken to the pyramids fell on him…you didn't, Senenmut, did you? You did! Your eyes always spoke more than your lips. You haven't changed a bit, have you?

SENENMUT: Of course not. Now tell me everything. I never told on you and you have no cause not to trust me.

MERITRE: That was because of pride and that was a long time ago. Only children can afford pride.

(Lights down on MERITRE and SENENMUT. Lights up on WANRE and TUTU as NEFERURE enters.)

NEFERURE: I have convinced my father to send for all the high priests. At dawn, he will decree before them that you are to be the next pharaoh. This will strengthen your claim to the throne when he's gone, so we have nothing to fear.

TUTU: How many times have I told you to knock?

NEFERURE: Did you hear what I said?

TUTU: Of course I'll be the next pharaoh, why do you think I married you?

NEFERURE: Well, you shouldn't be so sure, since you're not the direct descendent of a pharaoh. And my mother's slave girl Senenmut seems to be planning—

TUTU: Senenmut! Senenmut! Osiris damn that woman to the pit of the Devourer's stomach and you all with her! Do you expect me to fear an ignorant slave girl?! To cower before her, as you both seem to do! (To WANRE) Go to Syria! (To NEFERURE) And you! You think you've done a great deed by getting your father to promise that I will be the next pharaoh. That has been the assumption since we were married, Neferure.

At most, your mother will have some figurative title till she croaks, too. The lion eats the lamb and so our people cannot be lead by a woman. I don't want to hear another word, especially about some silly slave's fantasy. Slaves to me are as inconsequential as shadows.

(Lights shift to SENENMUT.)

SENENMUT: Meritre, I know people never treat you as they should. The way we ignore shadows, the entire world alive at our feet, until we need the shade. But whatever happens, I'll make sure that you are safe. I'll kill everyone in this palace, myself included, before I let them touch a hair on your head. You know I will. Now tell me everything.

Scene 5

(Setting: HATSHEPSUT's *room)*

SENENMUT: Hatshepsut.

HATSHEPSUT: Hatshepsut? You haven't called me that since the old days. In such a serious tone. Oh, say it again. Senenmut, it stirs old longings in me.

SENENMUT: Hatshepsut, I fear you will be happy no longer. Listen to me. At dawn, your husband plans to announce before high priests that Tutu won't need you as a regent and is ready to rule as pharaoh.

HATSHEPSUT: Thutmose wouldn't do that. He's too scared of me. Unless our daughter has gotten into him. That idiot! I'll kill him.

SENENMUT: You won't have to. I'll kill him. Tonight.

HATSHEPSUT: I meant "I'll kill him" as a figure of speech.

SENENMUT: I didn't. If we get rid of your husband right now, you will still be the regent. And once you are in power, it will be easy to proclaim yourself pharaoh.

HATSHEPSUT: The men in this world aren't going to allow that, Senenbutty.

SENENMUT: And what are you going to allow? Are you going to allow your husband—a man of no royal blood—to dictate what you do? Are you going to allow your son-in-law to have absolute power over you and take me for himself?

HATSHEPSUT: No. Let me think for a moment.

SENENMUT: We don't have a moment.

HATSHEPSUT: I said, let me think!

SENENMUT: As you wish, my Queen.

HATSHEPSUT: Enough with the "My Queen" business. You know it irritates me.

SENENMUT: Queen Hatshepsut, O royal one. Daughter of the gods, I am not worthy to be in your presence.

HATSHEPSUT: Senenmut. Stop it! It's so strange. We spend half of our lives trying to get power. And when we have it, we spend what's left of our lives looking for someone who would love us with or without it.

SENENMUT: You call what you have power! You're worse than me. You've got royal blood in your veins, but you're acting as if you were a slave! You, who the gods chose to rule by taking your brothers to the afterlife, had your right stolen from you. The world awaits you, crying out "we will not rest till the true pharaoh is on the throne!"

HATSHEPSUT: Yeah, yeah. Forget the bullshit. If we are to going to do this, what are we going to tell the people, you know the religious ones, so that they buy it?

SENENMUT: Tell the religious people… Hmmm, let me think of something good.

HATSHEPSUT: It better be, because if it is not, they'll revolt.

SENENMUT: They won't revolt. I'm telling you. I understand the people in a way that you cannot, because I am one of them. You get the peasants, say where I'm from, busy building a temple to Isis. And tell them they'll be blessed for doing so. You could do just about anything to them.

HATSHEPSUT: You better come up with something better than that.

SENENMUT: Okay. How about not only building a new temple, but telling the world the true story of your divine parentage? We'll have it written in stone that the god Amun saw the beauty of your mother. And was tempted and stole forth to her, like a panther, in the night.

HATSHEPSUT: You're getting warmer.

SENENMUT: When he found her asleep, he disguised himself as your father. And your mother believed the fragrant god, who kissed her till she woke, was her husband. Thus you are the child of amorous Amun. And your father, knowing his duty, entrusted you and only you with the royal position of pharaoh, even before your brothers died.

HATSHEPSUT: Yes. Yes!

SENENMUT: And the people shall, like your father, acclaim you king!

HATSHEPSUT: Yes, who will dare deny that I am a descendent of a god? Who will dare say my mother wasn't getting a little something-something from the great god Amun?

SENENMUT: No one. Give an unemployed man a job
and he'll believe you descended from a god, trust
me. Let me build for you a temple in the Valley of the
Kings.

HATSHEPSUT: Yes!

SENENMUT: And all who look upon it, generations
upon generations, will know and tell the story of
Hatshepsut, the woman who became pharaoh.

HATSHEPSUT: Yes! *(Pause)* Only we will not kill my
husband, but rather wait until he dies a natural death.
His pyramid is only half-built. The tomb within it isn't
even ready for him. He'll have a horrible afterlife.

SENENMUT: But, the priests are on their way.

HATSHEPSUT: So? I'll send word that my husband is too
ill for anyone to be admitted into his chamber and have
them barred from the palace gates. There is to be no
more talk of bloodshed, Senenmut. Against a pharaoh,
our god on earth—

SENENMUT: You are my god upon earth. I recognize no
other.

HATSHEPSUT: You are crazy with love for me. It is
endearing, but I can't allow you to entertain thoughts
of killing my husband.

SENENMUT: I will do as you wish. If you don't desire
it, I wouldn't dream of letting him die anything but a
natural death.

HATSHEPSUT: That's my girl. Leave it to nature. Let's go
eat, drink, and mix our scents and send love's perfume
to heaven. *(She exits.)*

SENENMUT: Of course, leave it to nature. *(Aside)* And
what are we but nature's most mean-spirited agents?

Scene 6

(SENENMUT *enters the bed-chamber of* THUTMOSE II. *He is resting and being fanned by* MERITRE. SENENMUT *motions* MERITRE *over to her.*)

SENENMUT: Hey, Moonbeam.

MERITRE: Hello, Noble Tutor Senenmut.

SENENMUT: Soon, you and I will eat rows and rows of grapes together, will we not?

MERITRE: I'm sure we shall. If you say so, Noble Tutor.

(SENENMUT *approaches the pharaoh who feels her eyes on him, sits up, and looks at her with dread.*)

SENENMUT: Dear pharaoh, oh great child of Osiris. I beg of you just a moment of your time. Alone.

THUTMOSE II: Please. Go away. I'll have none of your insults today.

SENENMUT: Insults from me, sire? Heaven forbid.

THUTMOSE II: Let's stay out of each other's hair. Do whatever you want. Tell Hatshepsut to let you do whatever you want, on my orders—

SENENMUT: Your orders? To Hatshepsut, sire?

THUTMOSE II: No! I don't mean that! Don't get me in trouble. I mean, you two work it out. Whatever this is, I want no part of it.

SENENMUT: No part of what, sire?

THUTMOSE II: Please leave me alone. Please go.

SENENMUT: But why, sire? Why do you start so?

THUTMOSE II: Do you want money?

SENENMUT: No! Sire, it is my honor just to serve you. What more can I ask for? I'm a simple peasant girl from Karnak. Now, call your people away so we may speak in private. (*Whispering to him*) I have fallen out of the Queen's favor. Take pity on me. I must have a word with you alone.

THUTMOSE II: I am not a hard man.

SENENMUT: We know.

THUTMOSE II: What?

SENENMUT: I mean, my liege, you are a million time more kind and generous than Queen Hatshepsut. So I trust you will lend me your ear in private?

THUTMOSE II: Well, I...

SENENMUT: Please, sire. O mighty pharaoh. Show pity on lowly me.

THUTMOSE II: All right. (*Speaking in a commanding voice*) I want to be alone with the tutor Senenmut.

(MERITRE *exits.*)

SENENMUT: Oh, thank you, my mighty pharaoh. I am here to beg you to help me.

THUTMOSE II: Get on your knees.

SENENMUT: (*Reluctantly obeys*) Queen Hatshepsut despises me and wishes me dead. She told me that she hated me because I could never love her the way I love you. Master, I have always loved you and you alone.

THUTMOSE II: Say it again.

SENENMUT: I have always loved you—

THUTMOSE II: No, no. Call me master again. How I've longed to hear you address me as such.

SENENMUT: O master. My master. Son of gods and light of this earth. O, mighty bull, who starts and smarts with desires given from the gods—

(SENENMUT *sneaks behind* THUTMOSE II, *attempting to stick a poison in his ear. He turns towards her and she hides the poison just in time.*)

THUTMOSE II: Oh, yes! It's happening! Yes! They said I was incapable, but Here. I. Go! *(Revealing himself to her)* Come here, slave-girl. I've wanted to do this to you for a long time.

(SENENMUT begins to back away and THUTMOSE II follows her throughout the next dialogue.)

SENENMUT: I've been a sworn virgin so long. I can't just do this, like our great love is merely dirty and common. We need pomp, circumstance, and a sort of funeral for my most private parts. Which you will bear through and tear asunder, like the moon burns a hole in the cloak of night!

THUTMOSE II: Come here!

SENENMUT: Please at least let me put something a little more…enticing on. So I can put us both in the right mood.

THUTMOSE II: I'm in the mood now, whore.

SENENMUT: Yes, call me all the right names. I feel so unworthy of being here. If only the girls in Karnak could see me now! Who would imagine me with a mighty pharaoh? But please make it easy on both of us. Close your eyes, Master! While I change for you, Sire!

THUTMOSE II: Okay, okay. *(muttering to himself)* Damn women.

SENENMUT: Stay very still. You will never spit in another mouth again.

THUTMOSE II: What?

(Before THUTMOSE II can move, SENENMUT sticks a poison in his ear. He writhes, unconscious on the floor.)

SENENMUT: Wow. I thought it would take more to kill a pharaoh. *(She goes to door in order to get MERITRE.)* The pharaoh is in an amorous mood. He calls for Meritre.

(MERITRE enters.)

SENENMUT: Queen's orders. She's taking over the throne. That will show him he should not have messed with the girls from Karnak.

MERITRE: I can't believe it. How many years I wished I could see him dying like this before me.

(MERITRE *kicks* THUTMOSE II. *Then she gets a better idea. She begins picking his pockets.*)

SENENMUT: Follow my lead and I'll explain the rest later. Can you make a few sounds as if you're making love?

MERITRE: You mean like this. Oh, pharaoh! Naughty pharaoh!

(MERITRE *makes sexual sounds while slipping rings off of* THUTMOSE II's *fingers. When she finds particularly exquisite pieces of jewelry, she gets even more excited.*)

SENENMUT: That sounds right. And maybe I'll be making those love sounds too. If Happy gets busy with the duties of the throne, and I am brave enough to risk it, the perfume of my love-making shall linger long after I leave these halls.

Scene 7

(HATSHEPSUT *is sitting alone crying.* SENENMUT *enters, hesitating at the door.*)

HATSHEPSUT: Come here, Senenmut.

SENENMUT: Why these tears? We have work to do. We must finish what nature started.

HATSHEPSUT: I never expected you to actually go through with it.

(HATSHEPSUT *cries in* SENENMUT's *arms.*)

SENENMUT: Through with what?

HATSHEPSUT: You said you wanted to kill my husband.

SENENMUT: Your husband died a natural death.

HATSHEPSUT: Really? You visited him in his chamber while I was asleep last night. Now, suddenly, he is dead.

SENENMUT: He was very sick, remember? And, who told you I was in his chamber?

HATSHEPSUT: I have obviously given you too much freedom. That's a mistake I intend to correct. You don't get to ask me questions. You get to answer mine. What did you do to my husband?

SENENMUT: Why don't you ask what he did to me?

HATSHEPSUT: Because he's the one who is dead.

SENENMUT: Look, Happy, I had hoped to spare you the ugliness of the full truth. But, if it is truth you want, then it's truth I'll give you. I went in to talk, merely talk, to your husband.

HATSHEPSUT: Why would you do that?

SENENMUT: I knew the priests were going to be here today. I knew they would be expecting a decree about who would be the next pharaoh. I foolishly, stupidly, and ignorantly went in to ask your husband if he would name you as that pharaoh.

HATSHEPSUT: What?

SENENMUT: I thought it would be a good idea. How wrong I was. You said you were willing to be the next pharaoh after him if we could manage to get the support of the people. I thought what better way to get the support of the people than to have your husband name you as the next ruler. Then, then, then…

HATSHEPSUT: Then what?

SENENMUT: I'm ashamed to say. Modesty prevents me.

(HATSHEPSUT *slaps* SENENMUT.)

HATSHEPSUT: You are not governed by the rules of modesty. You are governed by me. What happened in that chamber?

SENENMUT: What happened is your husband attacked me.

HATSHEPSUT: My husband?

SENENMUT: Yes, he most certainly did. It was horrible. In fact, it was so terrifying it made me forswear the touch of any man ever, any person even.

HATSHEPSUT: But he had been...incapable for years.

SENENMUT: That's why I felt safe being alone with him for just a few moments. To beg him for your sake in private. He said that seeing me supplicant before him made him a man again, bigger and badder than he was before. He told me that he coveted me from the first day you brought me to the palace.

HATSHEPSUT: Oh, that bastard!

SENENMUT: My tears angered him. He said my sniveling might make him grow impotent again. He had me call in a slave girl and told me to watch, listen, and learn how he liked it done.

HATSHEPSUT: Why did you not run?

SENENMUT: Because I could not. He commanded his guards to hold me down and keep my eyelids pressed open so I couldn't look away. I couldn't even blink.

HATSHEPSUT: Which of his guards? Call them in! They shall pay!

SENENMUT: For following orders? That's unjust. The guards wanted to help me. I could see in their eyes. But, they had to obey your husband's every foul command because he is...he was...

HATSHEPSUT: Pharaoh.

SENENMUT: He began by pushing, pushing, pushing the poor slave girl on the floor.

HATSHEPSUT: Okay, I don't really need to hear all this.

SENENMUT: Happy, he died on top of her. He died inside of her. And I had to watch. Please, please, Happy, have pity on me and protect from men. I've become like you. I don't want them ever to touch me.

HATSHEPSUT: Never fear. Never fear. I'd stop the flow of the Nile to keep you safe. You think I'd let a man, who I was capable of killing, hurt you?

SENENMUT: But how can you prevent that?

HATSHEPSUT: I, I can have anything I want.

SENENMUT: Only a pharaoh has absolute power. He gives me longing looks.

HATSHEPSUT: Who?

SENENMUT: The man your husband wanted to name as the next pharaoh, Tutu.

HATSHEPSUT: Tutu is not going to be the next pharaoh. I am.

Scene 8

(HATSHEPSUT *is planning her speech. She is dressed in the traditional male clothing that we have seen* THUTMOSE II *wearing, along with the gold beard and headdress.*)

HATSHEPSUT: …for that reason, I have been ordained pharaoh of this land. The great god saw the beauty of my mother and decided to take on the form of my father and come to her in the night. Do not doubt that the gods that cut out the circle of the sun in the sky and stenciled rainbows on the backs of every butterfly

could make a chaste woman big with their child. He
told my mother I would be lifted up and chosen to rule
Egypt and there I would grow to stand among gods
where ...where...where...

SENENMUT: Where my father before me....

HATSHEPSUT: Right. Okay. Where my father before me
and his father before him once stood.

SENENMUT: Right.

(NEFERURE *enters, dressed in mourning clothes.*)

NEFERURE: Mother, I need to talk to you. Why are you
dressed in Father's clothing?

SENENMUT: Because he is dead.

NEFERURE: As you shall soon be, when my husband
takes over the throne.

HATSHEPSUT: There is one crucial thing amiss in your
little plot, my daughter.

NEFERURE: Amiss?

HATSHEPSUT: Yes, amiss. Your husband is not going
to be the pharaoh. Not now, not ever. It will be I, and
after me, you.

NEFERURE: Mother, I need to speak to you alone.

HATSHEPSUT: Anything we say can and will be said in
front of your tutor.

SENENMUT: That's okay. I know when I'm not wanted. I
shall leave. But, as your tutor, let me teach you one last
lesson, my dear pupil. Don't fight with someone who
was born with nothing to lose. (*She kisses* HATSHEPSUT
passionately and exits.)

NEFERURE: You both disgust me.

HATSHEPSUT: I disgust you? And that husband of
yours, I'm supposed to believe he excites you?

NEFERURE: He is a decent man.

HATSHEPSUT: He is a fool. A fool who cares more about his silly garden than this kingdom.

NEFERURE: You chose him!

HATSHEPSUT: Even pharaohs make mistakes.

NEFERURE: Mother, you are not acting in accordance with respect for anything except your own selfish whims. Which I could forgive if they weren't borrowed desires, from a slave girl from Karnak!

HATSHEPSUT: Better to be born a slave with the heart of a royal than a royal who insists on being a slave.

NEFERURE: Those are her words. Senenmut is wrong when she goes around saying that she plays you like a lyre. She plays you like a flute, making her thoughts come through your lips.

HATSHEPSUT: So what if she supported my decision to do this? The kingship passed over my head to that of my husband's. Because he had a twig to twirl his crown on that I didn't. I am righting this wrong for the sake of the kingdom. Your kingdom. I waited to do this until your father died a natural death.

NEFERURE: A natural death?! How can you actually believe that?

HATSHEPSUT: Don't act like you miss him.

NEFERURE: He was my father and a decent man.

HATSHEPSUT: That doesn't mean you miss him. It's you and I here, Daughter. No one else. No need to lie about what he meant to you.

NEFERURE: This is not about my father. If you marry again and have a son, what will become of mine?

HATSHEPSUT: You don't even have any sons yet. Besides, I will not marry again.

NEFERURE: You will. When you tire of this slave girl. Mother, you cannot go against the customs of our people.

HATSHEPSUT: What will it cost you if I rule for a few years?

NEFERURE: What will it cost you to act in accordance with our ancient traditions?

HATSHEPSUT: Everything. You fool! You want to be queen when I am offering you the chance to be king. I am more than a pair of ovaries, more than a meeting ground where one king enters and another exits. And so are you. Can't you see? I'm doing this for you too, Daughter. And, if I succeed, I will have given you the greatest gift. Freedom. You will not like the life that is fit for a queen, you will find it hateful. I can promise you that. You must, my only daughter, take the power I'll give you with both hands. It will be your deliverance from a life I am sure you will not want.

NEFERURE: Mother, my husband is prepared to do anything to attain his right to rule as pharaoh. I cannot placate him.

HATSHEPSUT: Try.

NEFERURE: He will not listen.

HATSHEPSUT: He cannot win against me.

NEFERURE: My husband is savage in ways we women don't understand. Please back down. I fear for you.

Scene 9

(Setting: TUTU's *room.* HATSHEPSUT *can be heard giving the same speech from the earlier scene in the background.)*

TUTU: I said no!

NEFERURE: Really, Tutu. I can't believe you are letting her take over this kingdom. I'm truly very angry.

TUTU: It's not my concern. Let Hatshepsut do what she wants. Let her rule as regent until I am old enough.

NEFERURE: Listen. She's telling the people she should be regarded as pharaoh.

TUTU: That's just the rhetoric of a proud old woman. I'm young yet. I'm just a seed of the self that I will be soon, the grain that begets a pearl. I was not raised to be pharaoh. So I must be born anew and rear myself to rule this kingdom. I must seek knowledge, slow and deliberate as my sunflowers turn towards the light.

NEFERURE: She is out there giving a speech announcing that she is taking over the kingdom. Can't you do something?

(The crowds are roaring.)

TUTU: I don't want to do something. I'm not ready. Hatshepsut is old and not going to be around long anyway.

NEFERURE: How dare you say that about my mother?

TUTU: Oh, excuse me. I forgot your deep affection for her. How silly of me. She told me that she wished to rule for a few years. Until I am mature enough. And when I am, I will take the throne after her.

NEFERURE: And if she marries again?

TUTU: She will not. I will be pharaoh after Hatshepsut. When I am ready. So you can just…just…calm down! *(He storms off.)*

NEFERURE: I will not calm down. For a chance at being pharaoh, my mother forsakes a line of queens. Is it fair to raise me to be a queen, and then expect me to become a pharaoh? *(She prays)* Osiris, wake the river god of the Nile, like a new lover. Tease him into rising

and flooding this world with a short death, which will
bring us a new life. But—just in case you're busy to
do all that—let me find servants most suited for dark
deeds. Help me make them make the dams we built to
steady the Nile themselves be damned and eventually,
like shards, be splintered. Let the peasants believe
the floods are a sign of your displeasure with my
mother's rule. Give me courage to destroy the gardens
my husband loves, and let him blame it all upon
Senenmut. Do all I desire, and I will persecute every
fool who follows the cult of Isis and does not give their
due to you. I swear it.

Scene 10

(HATSHEPSUT *and* SENENMUT *are on-stage.*)

HATSHEPSUT: Isn't it absolutely lovely? Us being
together?

SENENMUT: Of course, Happy.

HATSHEPSUT: It is lovely. Say it back to me.

SENENMUT: It is—

HATSHEPSUT: No, no, no. Just the word. Lovely.

SENENMUT: Lovely.

HATSHEPSUT: Ah, loveliness calling out to its self. Do
you know what it sounds like to hear loveliness itself
speak and name its own name?

SENENMUT: Lovely.

HATSHEPSUT: You guessed it. It's been a nice six
months, has it not been?

SENENMUT: I would say so.

HATSHEPSUT: Our architects are drawing plan after plan for temples in my honor. But, I want to build a temple for you.

SENENMUT: I need no temples, my pharaoh.

HATSHEPSUT: Not even in Karnak? I can raze the market where you were sold and build one.

SENENMUT: Don't raze the market where I was sold. End slavery. Just kidding. You'd be thrown from power the next day if you tried to free slaves.

HATSHEPSUT: Would I?

SENENMUT: Absolutely. And the landowners and generals would use you being a woman as an excuse to do it. We can't afford to feed all those freed slaves. We would simply be making starvation their new master.

HATSHEPSUT: There must be some way we can do it.

SENENMUT: You have no idea what makes an empire an empire.

HATSHEPSUT: And you do?

SENENMUT: I know the price of food, which you do not. And I know how many people must be fed. We can make symbolic gestures. We can decree that the words of priestesses on religious law matter as much as the words of priests. That won't ruffle too many feathers. But, basically, we must keep things as they are.

HATSHEPSUT: As they are? What is the point of me—a woman—being in power if I rule exactly as men before me have ruled? I wanted to be pharaoh so nothing could ever be done to me or to the ones I loved. But, now that I am in power, I can actually think about what I can do to others. For others!

SENENMUT: Would it be so wrong if we just accepted that we women are no better and no worse than men?

And we don't have to pretend to be, in order to expect all the rights they have?

HATSHEPSUT: Yes, it would. I will look into how much it will cost to free slaves, Senenmut.

(There is a knocking at the door.)

HATSHEPSUT: No interruptions!

SERVANT: *(Off)* It is important, O pharaoh.

SENENMUT: I'll decide that. Speak your important words from where you are.

SERVANT: *(Off)* But…but…the peasants are crowding the palace walls. The dams have burst.

HATSHEPSUT: The dams have burst?! That's impossible.

SERVANT: *(Off)* Most of Karnak and the surrounding towns have been wiped out.

SENENMUT: Karnak?

SERVANT: *(Off)* Including…including the Great Tutor Senenmut's entire family. According to rumor.

SENENMUT: My family? I can't believe it.

HATSHEPSUT: Are you all right, Senenmut?

SENENMUT: My entire family? Gone?

HATSHEPSUT: It appears so.

SENENMUT: You should go comfort the people.

HATSHEPSUT: First, I must comfort you. You, who means more to me than the whole world—

SENENMUT: It will look bad if you don't go comfort the people.

HATSHEPSUT: Yes, but are you all right?

SENENMUT: Why certainly. Now I don't have to feel guilty about not sending the bastards back home any money. *(Struggling not to cry)* What did they ever do

for me but beat me and sell me the first chance they
got? Maybe I could forgive them if they gained all
the power in heaven, all the gold in Egypt, or a love
beyond comprehension. *(She regains her composure quick
as a snap.)* But they sold me for the price of a meal,
and a cheap meal at that! Now when you address the
people, be sure to say—

HATSHEPSUT: But your family…it seems so cruel to not
even acknowledge—

SENENMUT: If it's cruel to live for you and you alone,
then I am cruel. Happy, you must go and address the
people.

HATSHEPSUT: What should I say to them?

SENENMUT: Tell them that their families have joined the
crew of the Sun Boat that rides across the sky. That the
laughter of the living is the breath that fuels its flames
so, when we are of cheer, the dead are more bright,
more near. That the moon is the eye through which the
dead take turns looking upon the living, and they use it
to light our way with love. That in the moments when
you think you are most alone, the ones you knew come
and kiss you through raindrops. And though those
who have left us are forever shouting 'I am near to
where you are!' we can almost hear them whisper 'I'm
not so very far' if we pause and listen to the rhythms in
the rush of our river.

HATSHEPSUT: That's quite good. I almost believe it.

SENENMUT: Good, it will make you more convincing.
And be sure to tell them that this obviously was the
work of the Hyksos still living among us. It is always
easier to brook pain if you have someone else to blame.

HATSHEPSUT: But it's not those Hyksos' fault. Many of
them have been living here for generations.

SENENMUT: Would you rather they blamed us?

(TUTU *enters.*)

HATSHEPSUT: What are you doing here? Entering without my permission.

TUTU: There has been a massacre.

HATSHEPSUT: We've heard about the dam.

TUTU: No, someone destroyed my gardens. Cut off the heads of my lotus blossoms! And my newly planted trees! I can't even talk about what they did to my trees! They were just seedlings.

HATSHEPSUT: I don't care about your stupid gardens. There have been entire towns wiped out by the flood. I have to go speak to the people.

TUTU: What? How could you not care?

SENENMUT: *(To* HATSHEPSUT*)* Tell him we'll pay for the reconstruction of his ridiculous gardens.

TUTU: *(Turning towards* SENENMUT*)* The servants say that you, Senenmut, are responsible!

SENENMUT: What? Now, Sire, why would I want to destroy your gardens?

TUTU: Because you are jealous of Wanre's love for me.

SENENMUT: I love no one but my pharaoh.

TUTU: But who is the pharaoh in the kingdom of your hard, beating heart? Evil, vile woman! I'm going to tell everything that you've done.

HATSHEPSUT: You are not still that man's plaything. I thought we beheaded him long ago.

TUTU: She had another man killed and gave you his head instead. I know this. Wanre himself wrote and told me.

HATSHEPSUT: So you do still love him!

SENENMUT: No! I didn't Wanre killed because I feel bad for his family. For that reason alone.

TUTU: Then, why did you give orders for his wife's death? Wanre still doesn't know about it and no one has the heart to tell him. I've ordered Wanre back here from Syria, so I can break the news gently. He's waiting for me in my chamber, and I can't face him!

HATSHEPSUT: I cannot control what lives in your heart, though I have tried, but I can decide who lives on this earth. Your precious Wanre will not live another day longer for you to love and to torment me with.

TUTU: You will not touch a hair on Wanre's head.

HATSHEPSUT: I will not touch a hair on his head, but I'll stick a stake in that heart that dared to love what I love.

TUTU: I'll decide that. I am old enough to rule as pharaoh now, Hatshepsut.

HATSHEPSUT: And you have been for years. However, I am the pharaoh. It is my right by birth. All Egyptians recognize me as such.

TUTU: You said you only wished to rule as regent. But now I see that you have taken every step to ensure that you and you alone reign over Egypt! You have taken the kingship and I have stood by and watched.

HATSHEPSUT: And?

TUTU: And I defended you when others laughed at you for dressing like a man, giving yourself the title of the great bull, when you so clearly are not. I waited to assume power so I could learn how to be a worthy pharaoh, more worthy than those before me. Now, you want to rob me of life's most precious treasure, the chance to fail. How much finer to fail as a pharaoh than to succeed at anything less! I will take my right to rule back from you, Hatshepsut! Soon I'll wipe out every trace of this abomination. No one will know of the woman who fooled Egypt into believing she was a true pharaoh.

HATSHEPSUT: Really? I don't think so. I'll order my guards to kill you.

TUTU: And I'll tell them 'By the light of the sun-god Re and the true pharaoh, I forbid you to take another step. Does she look like a pharaoh? Or sound like a god among us that might make the earth shudder?' And because I am a man, they will recognize me as the true pharaoh.

HATSHEPSUT: I am the true pharaoh.

TUTU: I am the true pharaoh.

SENENMUT: Kill him yourself, Happy. Before this gets out of hand.

(HATSHEPSUT *slides out her dagger.*)

HATSHEPSUT: I will kill him. *(Calls to servants offstage)* Bring me the scribe Wanre immediately. He's next, after I finish off this lotus-lover.

(HATSHEPSUT *begins to back an unarmed* TUTU *into a corner.* WANRE *enters.*)

WANRE: What has happened?

SENENMUT: They are fighting. I've missed you. All of you!

WANRE: *(Ignoring* SENENMUT*)* Come on, Your Highnesses. This is horrible. No unnecessary bloodshed among the royals. Stop! Let the little people get all sweaty and bloody. You two don't need to physically fight to settle this. Why are servants made to serve you, except in times like these? Let us start a civil war instead. It is more civilized.

SENENMUT: And tear our country apart?! No. It is more humane to let these two fight it out. For the sake of the kingdom.

HATSHEPSUT: No, Senenmut. I'm not afraid of this banana-backed tutu of a man. But the scribe does have a point.

WANRE: So, shall I give the order for war?

TUTU: I will agree if Hatshepsut agrees.

HATSHEPSUT: Yes, that sounds reasonable.

WANRE: Then let both of you gather your forces together to battle at dawn. We'll meet here at sunup to watch. This is the best view from the palace. We'll watch together whom the gods favor, like the civilized people we are. Agreed?

TUTU: Agreed.

(HATSHEPSUT *stares at* SENENMUT, *who shakes her head "no".*)

HATSHEPSUT: Agreed.

Scene 11

(*It is still night.* SENENMUT *follows* WANRE *onto the stage.*)

WANRE: Stop following me!

SENENMUT: Come here.

WANRE: No.

SENENMUT: Come here and be sure to bring all of you with you. Oh, by the way, sorry about your wife.

WANRE: My wife?

SENENMUT: You didn't hear about...the accident?

WANRE: The accident? (*Enraged and about to hit* SENENMUT)

SENENMUT: One scream from me and you're as good as dead. You don't want to make your poor motherless children orphans.

WANRE: When our people win tomorrow, I'm going to crack your neck like a chicken. You are so evil. So evil. My poor, beautiful wife...she didn't deserve this.

SENENMUT: You couldn't have liked her all that much. Why else would you have been so eager to leave her side for me?

WANRE: Is nothing sacred to you? You foulest cohort of Seth, you snake!

SENENMUT: It's not like I killed your children.

WANRE: You crazy whore! My wife!

(HATSHEPSUT *stands in the doorway, unnoticed by* SENENMUT.)

SENENMUT: You know, you should have let them fight it out. She would have won. The tiresome old hag is stronger than she looks. Go back to Syria tonight and I'll send for you when it's safe.

WANRE: I'll stay and take my chances. Your side may lose.

SENENMUT: What would it matter? My love, I could wrap Tutu around my finger just as easily as I do Happy if I needed to.

(HATSHEPSUT *steps forward and faces* SENENMUT.)

SENENMUT: *(Seeing her)* Happy!

WANRE: You got yourself in a load of shit now. Bye, bye, Senenmut. *(Exits laughing)*

HATSHEPSUT: Even this am I not spared?

SENENMUT: Happy, I—

HATSHEPSUT: Silence! Now I know why the heart is cut into chambers! So we don't give it to ungrateful people whole!

SENENMUT: Happy, don't insist upon making yourself miserable. If we could hear everything that was said behind our backs, we wouldn't have one friend or lover left in the world. Look, I am not the nicest person around. I have some flaws. But, ingratitude is not one of them. You've been good to me. I know that. I really never meant to hurt you.

HATSHEPSUT: Enough! Why is it when we do cruel things to others, we are called 'inhuman'? And when we do cruel things to ourselves, we are called 'in love'?

SENENMUT: I love you with as much love as my heart can contain. Is it fair to curse the cup you drink from because it can't hold enough to quench your thirst? For it gives you all it can. I beg you to see it this way and it will be easier for you, my pharaoh.

HATSHEPSUT: Some of my viziers have aligned themselves with Tutu. My wisest ones.

SENENMUT: We will not lose. I did not sneak away to meet Wanre. I met him by chance. I left our bed to enlist the help of women, the high priestesses who believe in the righteousness of your rule. They have agreed to follow my orders and most of Egypt follows theirs. They're rallying their most radical devotees by the thousands. The strongest of them will join our men on the battlefield.

HATSHEPSUT: And if they fail us, these women?

SENENMUT: We still won't lose.

HATSHEPSUT: Why not?

SENENMUT: Because I didn't get this far to lose now.

Scene 12

(The dawn is breaking. WANRE, SENENMUT, TUTU, and NEFERURE have assembled. WANRE walks by SENENMUT, avoiding SENENMUT.)

SENENMUT: Don't worry. I'll have my fill of you soon enough.

WANRE: After we win, just remember. Crack. Like a chicken.

SENENMUT: After we win, I will be merciful to you. Or maybe I won't. You should never trust a woman you have wronged.

WANRE: How have I wronged you? You forced me into exile, killed my wife, and you say I have wronged you. How have I wronged you? Answer me! How have I wronged you?

SENENMUT: By not loving me back. And I will make you pay for it when we win. I'm going to have you chained and shackled and the only person you will see for the rest of your life is me.

(HATSHEPSUT *enters, looking tired.*)

NEFERURE: Mother…

HATSHEPSUT: Do not speak to me. Let us simply watch.

(*A horn is blown. They watch the audience as if they were a battlefield.*)

SENENMUT: Look at them, lined up!

TUTU: There they are.

NEFERURE: They look like they're ready to tear one another apart.

HATSHEPSUT: Oh, no, Imwansut…he was struck. Get up, poor fool! I know your mother! She would want you to get up.

SENENMUT: Never mind him. There are others.

WANRE: Is that Tellamum?

TUTU: I can't tell. They all look the same.

HATSHEPSUT: *(To* SENENMUT*)* Come here. Where are the women?

SENENMUT: They're out there. They are biding their time. They won't fail us.

NEFERURE: What are you talking about, what women?

SENENMUT: The women.

TUTU & WANRE: Go, Tellamum! GO! GO! GO! *(They continue watching and cheering as if at a sporting event.)*

WANRE: Where is Isis, the great goddess to save you now, Senenmut?

SENENMUT: Speak against those whose wrath you can handle, fool. Isis has more important affairs to attend to.

WANRE: You can say that again.

SENENMUT: But she will imbue every woman in every village with the power to come and fight for our rights.

NEFERURE: I think she's losing it. *(To* SENENMUT*)* You enlisted the women? To kill their brothers and sons?

WANRE: Hey, Sire, get a load of this.

TUTU: Wanre, leave me alone. I'm watching the battle.

SENENMUT: They will come. For the sake of their sisters and daughters, they will come. And you will be sorry. The greatest pharaoh knows that they will come. She knows! Happy, the women will come, won't they?

HATSHEPSUT: I hope so. For their sakes as well as ours.

TUTU: Look, your side is fleeing! Like rabbits! Look at them go!

*(*WANRE *and* TUTU *laugh, whooping with joy and clapping. Through the next speech,* HATSHEPSUT *takes a vial of poison and mixes it with wine in a cup.* TUTU *and* WANRE *watch her mix it.* SENENMUT *still watches the battlefield and* NEFERURE *watches* SENENMUT.*)*

SENENMUT: Wait! Nobody move. It's not over. Wait for
the women. They'll come. Yes, ma'am. I'm going to bet
on the women. Where are the women who said they
would come and fight? Where are the women?

NEFERURE: The bitch has gone mad.

SENENMUT: *(quieter)* Because if you don't rise up
together now, then you deserve everything you get.

HATSHEPSUT: They aren't coming, Senenmut.

SENENMUT: They said they would. They promised me.

HATSHEPSUT: They lied, sweet Senenmut. *(She drinks the
poison.)*

SENENMUT: No, I know they weren't lying. People who
lie know when others are lying.

HATSHEPSUT: I have taken a poison.

SENENMUT: No.

HATSHEPSUT: Hold me, Senenmut. *(To* NEFERURE*)*
Daughter, treat my body according to how you would
want your daughter to treat yours. You will have no
sons. Only daughters, as loyal to you as you are to
me. That's my last words to you. *(To Tutu)* Thutmose,
do not harm those who followed me. Remember
everything I did, I did alone.

TUTU: I am just, Queen Hatshepsut.

SENENMUT: Pharaoh Hatshepsut! Know that I have
loved you! Not in the way you needed me to, maybe,
but I have loved you!

HATSHEPSUT: Listen to me, Sweet One. Now that
the whirlwind of my days has spun its last turn,
knowing how unshakable my trust was in you, how
deep my love was for you, I now realize…I went a bit
overboard. I did. But I won't correct my mistake now.
Maybe the mistakes we make are not mistakes. They
are the only ways we know how to live. You made it

so that the end of my life doesn't have to mean the end of my story. I didn't become a pharaoh because I loved you. I loved you because you believed I deserved to be a pharaoh. *(She dies.)*

NEFERURE: My mother is dead. I can't believe she is dead.

(SENENMUT tries to sneak away.)

WANRE: Where do you think you're going?

NEFERURE: *(Pointing to SENENMUT)* You did this!

SENENMUT: You cursed her while she was alive, don't pretend to love her while she is dead! She hates you and will haunt you forever!

WANRE: The moment we've all been waiting for. What should we do to her first?

SENENMUT: You bastards think you are going to get me. Don't you know Isis has given me the power to disappear?!

(SENENMUT does a crazy dance. The rest are stunned for a moment. However, SENENMUT does not disappear.)

SENENMUT: Well, it was worth a shot.

(They surround her.)

WANRE: Nice try.

NEFERURE: Let me tear out her eyes.

TUTU: No. No need for excess savagery. It wouldn't look good.

WANRE: But she's the cause of this war. It is she that ruled while Hatshepsut reigned.

NEFERURE: Show her no mercy, Tutu! Let's cut through her bones. Like she cut through your trees. Down the middle.

TUTU: I disposed of my trees. Alone. How did you know they were cut down the middle?

NEFERURE: I, I…I didn't know…I was told…by…

TUTU: I will deal with you later, Neferure.

SENENMUT: It would be best to dispose quickly of such a wife.

NEFERURE: Silence! We're going to shut you up for good. And you won't get beheading. We're going to cut off your breasts and rape you with knives!

WANRE: Let me take care of her. I'll just crack her neck like a chicken. Quick and easy.

TUTU: Enough. She shall live, as all Hatshepsut's followers will. And owe me thanks for letting them live.

WANRE: Everyone except her. Why are you doing this, Your Highness?

NEFERURE: I know why! She is to work in your harem.

TUTU: Perhaps. Or some other position fitting her low station in life.

WANRE: She is too dangerous, Your Highness.

SENENMUT: If you don't kill me, Tutu, I'll kill you. By Pharaoh Hatshepsut's honor, I swear it.

WANRE: See, it would be unwise. Give her the same poison Queen Hatshepsut drank. At least, we'll make her worse nightmare come true. She often said the only thing she feared was dying a virgin.

TUTU: Then let her die a virgin.

(WANRE *prepares the poison for her.*)

SEMENMUT: The truth of the matter is—

(WANRE *drops the poison and cracks her neck.*)

WANRE: No! Come back! Come back so I can kill you again! So I can dream about killing you again!

(WANRE *takes out a knife to stab the body of* SENENMUT, *but* TUTU *stops him.*)

TUTU: That's enough, Wanre. What's come over you?

WANRE: Sorry, I just wanted to make sure she's dead.

TUTU: She is. Let them both rot together!

NEFERURE: What do you mean? My mother is going into her temple and being wrapped and buried like the queen that she is.

TUTU: That is more than she deserves.

NEFERURE: Listen, Tutu.

TUTU: It's the great pharaoh Thutmose III you are speaking to. Address me as such.

NEFERURE: Listen, Tutu. Just remember that I am the daughter of Thutmose II and you are a pharaoh only because you are married to me.

TUTU: And?

NEFERURE: And so I ask you, my mighty God on earth, humbly for only one thing and that is to bury my mother, the daughter and wife of a pharaoh, in the fashion I choose.

WANRE: It is better to lay Queen Hatshepsut to a worthy rest.

TUTU: That's the only thing you ask?

NEFERURE: Yes. I do not want her spirit wandering the earth, with no place to rest. It will haunt our happiness together.

TUTU: Bury your mother.

NEFERURE: Thank you, O wise pharaoh.

TUTU: And let her name be buried with her. I'll give
the order and Hatshepsut will be stripped from all the
lists of pharaohs, as if she never existed. Scratch out
the eyes of all her statues and sphinxes, so she cannot
look upon the living world that I now reign over. Let
all record of her rule be blotted out as well as any
image of her. Except those of her as Queen Hatshepsut,
standing forever behind her father or her husband.
Not a word of protest, all you asked was the chance
to bury the body. No one will ever know the story of
Hatshepsut.

Epilogue

(NEFERURE *is on-stage.* WANRE *enters.*)

WANRE: Greetings, my Queen.

NEFERURE: Oh, Wanre. It's good to see you. I've just
finished the funeral rites for my mother and am so
tired. Have you done what I asked?

WANRE: Of course. I'm here to inform you that the
dams have all been put back in perfect order, my
Queen.

NEFERURE: Is that all?

WANRE: And we have caught those who said the dam's
destruction was by your order.

NEFERURE: And?

WANRE: They are dead as well as those who claim to
have heard them say it.

NEFERURE: Good. I will not forget your loyal service,
Wanre.

WANRE: May I return to my village now, my Queen?

NEFERURE: Yes, go to your children. But visit us soon.
Very soon.

WANRE: As soon as the Pharaoh asks for me. I am the Pharaoh's obedient servant.

NEFERURE: Yes. And I am hoping you and I will get closer as well. I need a friend.

WANRE: I am the Pharaoh's obedient servant.

(Pause)

NEFERURE: I see. Run along then.

WANRE: Good-bye, my Queen.

(WANRE exits. Then TUTU enters with MERITRE.)

NEFERURE: Tutu, who is this?

TUTU: Call me pharaoh.

NEFERURE: Pharaoh, who is this?

TUTU: A friend, dear. Goodnight.

NEFERURE: Where are you going?

TUTU: To my bedchamber.

NEFERURE: To our bedchamber? With the slave?

TUTU: Is there a problem with that?

NEFERURE: A minor one. Where am I supposed to sleep?

(Pause. MERITRE whispers something in TUTU's ear.)

TUTU: What a brilliant idea! You really are a quick girl, aren't you? *(To NEFERURE)* How about in the east wing?

NEFERURE: My mother's chamber?

TUTU: Of course. After all, it is fit for a queen.

END OF PLAY

AFTERWORD

I wrote FIT FOR A QUEEN while in graduate school. It is, in some ways, my first full-length play. I wrote it at a point when I was profoundly disillusioned with politics in general and the activists I knew in particular, most especially myself.

I had begun to see everything anyone did as a ploy for power and attention. The professors, intellectuals, and student speakers at rallies for causes I cared about seemed like wanna-demagogues, preaching to the converted for their own aggrandizement. When I was asked to speak, I too felt like a wannabe-demagogue who cared more about how I came off than what I actually accomplished.

It seemed myopically cruel to organize conferences about refugees at Ivy League colleges and end them by blowing a ton of our university's money on fancy meals for our invited speakers and ourselves. Yet, how I enjoyed those meals!

I questioned why I cared about the causes I did, and not others, and what it said about me.

I began to feel like humans were incapable of truly loving other people—that the only way we could co-exist with anyone at all is if we somehow saw some others (whether it is our family or our tribe or our nation) as extensions of ourselves, and therefore worthy of protection, nurturing, and love.

In other words, we mistook others for ourselves rather than truly cared about others.

These feelings were deeply at odds with that part of me that I knew also existed—the part of me that recognized nothing I did in a day made me feel better than standing up in a subway car for someone who needed to sit down. That part of me that hungered to be a kind person more than I yearned to be seen as a talented, famous, or smart one. That part of me that understood that the reason being kind is so important is because it is the only thing all of us can be.

I wrote FIT FOR A QUEEN at a time when I was deeply unsettled. My world didn't feel comic or tragic. It was coming at me as always both at the time. I aimed to create a play that reflected that sense of dislocation.

In the play, I changed the gender of Hatshepsut's favorite underling, Senenmut, from male to female. I also shortened Hatshepsut's reign from over twenty years to six months.

Incidentally, it took me twenty years after I wrote FIT FOR A QUEEN to find the right home for this tale of an African woman who ruled the superpower of the ancient world. I am deeply grateful to Colman Domingo for championing this play for over a decade and for introducing it to Ty Jones, Artistic Director of the Classical Theatre of Harlem. Thank you to Ty, David Roberts, and the entire inspired and inspiring C T H team. I am forever indebted to the director Tamilla Woodward, cast, and crew for lovingly taking on the telling of this story just days before the 2016 election in America, a country that—unlike ancient Egypt—has still never managed to have a woman in its highest office.

There are many reasons why a play by a woman of color glorifying, highlighting, and reveling in the fantastical history of regal people of color might have a hard time getting seen on an American stage. Not all are reasons you might expect. A producer who was keen on doing FIT FOR A QUEEN early in my career abruptly dropped the project after she visited the Egyptian collection at the Met, and realized I hadn't stuck more closely to the historical record. That damn Met! With all its damn truth always on display! It outs you every time.

It's been said that we lie three times on average per every ten minutes of conversation.

That means we are incapable of telling a simple story about the most mundane occurrence in our day without embellishing, exaggerating, and outright fabricating.

Why do we do that, Friends? To make our perspective—the real point of the story—clearer.

The facts in FIT FOR A QUEEN that are "true" are the aspects of this woman's story that mattered most to me. When Hatshepsut died, her son-in-law Thutmose III took over and not her daughter. He decreed that every monument and statue of her dressed as a pharaoh was to be destroyed, and most were. He had Hatshepsut's name stripped from the lists of rulers as if her reign never existed. He intended to allow only images of her as a wife and daughter, standing forever behind her husband or her father, to remain for eternity.

But, the smashed statues of Pharaoh Hatshepsut were painstakingly reconstructed three thousands years later. Her (and her people's) true history was unearthed in what is arguably one of the biggest triumphs of modern archeology.

A curator once told me there is something distinctive about all the statues of Pharaoh Hatshepsut that makes them recognizable to the trained eye. She is always smiling.

There is something quite fun about hearing the character of Thutmose III declare, "No one will know the story of Hatshepsut!" in a play about Hatshepsut.

Stories aren't like people. You can't kill them. Trying to do so only makes you a buffoon.

She got the last laugh.

—Betty Shamieh

CPSIA information can be obtained
at www.ICGtesting.com
Printed in the USA
LVHW040132270719
625586LV00006B/43/P

9 780881 457636